To! Aubrey

Thanks for suppor
and I just want you to know
that you are "AWESOME!!"
I wish that you prosper in
everything that you do. Congrats
in advance on your book. Many
Blessings!

THE LIFE
of an
OVERCOMER

THE LIFE
of an
OVERCOMER

The Life Story of
RETIRED COMMAND SERGEANT MAJOR
RODWELL L. FORBES, JR.
as told by
LISA R. RHODES

XULON PRESS ELITE

Xulon Press Elite
2301 Lucien Way #415
Maitland, FL 32751
407.339.4217
www.xulonpress.com

Unless otherwise indicated, Scripture quotations taken from the King James
Version (KJV) – *public domain*.

Printed in the United States of America.

ISBN-13: 978-1-54566-092-8

To my mom, Johnnie Mae Forbes: As I reflect on our time spent together, it is filled with so many wonderful memories. You brought out the best in me and would not allow me to keep my head down in any situation. I thank you for spending the time to raise and "Love" me with no restrictions. I am a better man because of you, and I just want you to know, "Job Well Done!" Rest in peace, until we meet again in Glory.

To my wife, Patricia a.k.a. (Sweet "P"): I am so blessed to have you in my life and to call you my "Best Friend." You've stood by my side for the good, bad, and indifferent. I believe we have become stronger and my love for you grows deeper. I am so elated on what the future holds, and I'm cherishing the present time that I have with you right now. One thing I do know is that "The Best Is Yet to Come," especially since it's with you. I love you, Sweet "P."

To my children, Vandale, Tisha, and Shauna, and my grandchildren: I am so proud to be called your "Dad" and "Papa" and have the privilege to be a part of your lives. As I watch each of you grow and develop into the men and women God created you to be and diligently raise your children, it just about brings tears to my eyes. I pray for God's bountiful Blessings on each one of you and your families and look forward to what God has in store for you.

ACKNOWLEDGEMENTS

I JUST WOULD LIKE TO TAKE THIS TIME TO ACKNOWL-
edge the family, friends, and people who have helped shape my life into
who I am today. First of all, I would like to thank my dad, who chal-
lenged me to do things he didn't even think I could accomplish. I'm
so proud to be Rodwell Jr. You've taught me how to make sacrifices
for your family no matter what it took. My siblings, Rebecca, Tonya,
Archie, Gregory, and Ephrim, I'm so proud to call you family, and if
I were to tell our story, that would be another book, maybe in the near
future. My brother-in-laws, Charles and William Dumas. My children,
Ralph and Erica Hankerson, La'Tisha and Brandon Early, La'Shauna
Free, I'm so thankful you all are in my life, and I look forward to what
is yet ahead in this life journey. My grandchildren, Angela, Josiah,
Jeremiah, Shamond, Jada, Layla, Brandy, Amana, Isaiah, Serenity, I
love you all! My grandparents, I love and miss you dearly, and I will
always remember the times you took us in for the summer with our
cousins and just loved on us. Grandpa Williams and Aunt Laura, thank
you for loving on me and teaching me valuable lessons about this life
that was yet to come. Let's take a walk back down memory lane starting
from my youth. My aunts and uncles, Aunt Jeanette, Auntie Barbara
and Big Larry, Aunt Lorraine and Uncle Johhny Boy, Aunt Ann, Uncle
Sammy Lee, thanks for always being there for me. My Cousins, Johnny

Parker, Lil' Larry, Kevin, Keith Hart, Belford, Brian, Peter, Michael, Satreena, Manee, Glen, Christy, Edward Bunch, Melissa, Charlene, Kendra, it was great growing up with you all and sharing life experiences. My nephews, Frederick and Jonathan Clark, Antwan Gibson, Lil' Greg, and Jovon. I would like to thank Roslyn Frazier, Tamika Bates, Stephanie, Cricket, and the Massa Family for always being there for support for Ephrim and I. Brian Young and Edwin Mcgee, who have been great friends since elementary school, our bond still remains strong today. Roderick Wright and family, who have been like my biological family, I'm so thankful to have you in my life. Gerald Bunch, we've been through a lot together, and you are closer to me than a cousin could ever be. Thanks for always being there for me. Yuri Chapman, thanks for pushing me like none other; you helped me become a better athlete and man. Coach Al Nastaci, you saw something in me that I didn't see in myself, and you never let me give up. You were like my father who encouraged me when I was down and gave me the boot when I needed it. Mr. and Mrs. Holmes, thanks for taking me in as one of your sons and helping my mom raise a young man. I pray for many "Bountiful Blessings" to you and your family. To our 1990 state Track and Field team winners, Robert Thomas, Red O'Laughlin, and Gerald Bunch, great job on putting it all together to win the state championship.

To my cousin Michael Jackson, thanks for believing in me and helping me get on my feet and taking me in as a doorman at the Hilton and a security guard at the Flamingo Casino. Your mentorship has always been invaluable. To my fellow marines at 2nd Marine Air Wing, Cherry Point, NC. Tommy Oatis and Byron Mouton, it was great serving with you both. To my friends at 7-1 Aviation Battalion/2-1 Aviation Battalion in Katterbach, Germany. CSM John Moore, 1SG John Alvey, Gemar and Tora Ridley, CPL Robinson, JJ and Ingrid Tighe, Darcy

Saint-Amant, Buzz, David Walther, Commo Dawgs, and Lafonte Beverly. Roderick Carter, thanks for always pushing me by leading from the front and being a close friend all the way through our military junctures. 2/502nd Air Assault Infantry Division, 4th Brigade Combat Team, 101st Air Assault Division, 525th Battlefield Surveillance Brigade, 586th Signal Company, Fort Bragg, North Carolina, Hampton University SROTC, Sergeants Major Academy Class 61, El Paso, Texas, 72nd Expeditionary Signal Battalion, Schweinfurt, Germany and Fort Meade, Maryland. To the Hospice of Chesapeake and Gilchrest, Diane Sancillio, Mary Jermann, Ben and all of the staff. It has been a pleasure working with you and getting to know you better. To all of the veterans who served from WWI to now, you are a major reason why I wrote this book. You mean that much to me, and I want you to get the help you so rightfully deserve. Thanks to everyone who supported me in this life journey, and it has truly been an honor to serve with each one of you. To my siblings, Archie and Laura Aples, Rebecca and Keith Gasper, Tonya Savice, Gregory Aples, and Ephrim Forbes. We have lived a very eventful life, and I do believe our best years are yet ahead of us. To all of our spiritual children, Melissa and Kenisha, you both have a special place in my heart. Robert and Katrina Elbert, Rio, Jessie, Nicole, and Kenny, thanks for being a part of my life. To my pastors, Steve and Barbara Jackson, Abundant Grace Church (AGC) El Paso, Texas, Kelvin and Regina Williamson, Rivers of Life Christian Church (ROLCC) Fayetteville, North Carolina, thanks for always having a listening ear and radiating the love of Christ in everything that you do and say. It truly means a lot to me. To my next-door neighbors, Glenn and Tammy, what a blessing to get to know you and call you both friends. Lastly, Lisa Rhodes who did all of the interviews and put it all together. Thanks for investing in me, and I pray for Bountiful Blessings to you and your family. Lastly, the Four Horsemen, Archie, Will, Gill and Steve, my brothers for life, let's continue to ride strong "Together!"

Chapter One

THE OVERCOMER

I WAS BORN ON JULY 29, 1971 IN NEW ORLEANS. FOR the first four years of my life, my family lived in the Desire projects. It was not uncommon to hear people engaging in gun fights and knife stabbings. Yet despite the violence, the all-black neighborhood was a close-knit community. I wasn't fearful in that environment. What I saw was just a way of life.

We were not a totally committed Christian family, but my parents instilled the values of hard work and the pursuit of a higher education. My father (and my namesake), Rodwell Lincoln Forbes Sr., worked as a merchant marine and was seldom home due to long deployments. Although my father hailed from Honduras, Spanish was rarely spoken in our home. My mother, Johnnie Mae Forbes, worked as a nurse assistant in the radiology/oncology department at what was then Charity Hospital. She was a native of New Orleans and the most influential person in my life.

My experience in the neighborhood was limited. As the second youngest of six children, I learned about the latest happenings from my two older sisters, Rebecca Marie Gasper and Tonya Marie Savice, and my two older brothers, Archie Lee Aples and Gregory David Aples.

They were very influential in my life and looked after me while my mother worked. My younger brother, Ephrim Richard Forbes, came five years after me.

When I was four years old, my father moved our family to Metairie, a predominately Caucasian community. We were one of only two black families in the neighborhood. My father moved us because he wanted the peace of mind and comfort of knowing that we would have better opportunities to advance in our education and our pursuit of a promising, competitive career.

The new neighborhood was a rude awakening. It was foreign to me. The adults were standoffish, and my siblings and I were estranged from our white classmates in school.

I can remember being chased home by white children after school. I attended Airline Park Elementary School and was a quiet kid. Initially, I wasn't one to fight back because my older brothers looked out for me. They excelled in sports, particularly track and field, so they tried to break the ice with their white classmates through athletics.

But eventually, I had to learn how to stand up for myself to defend my mother and Ephrim.

My most vivid memories of that time of my life are of the Ku Klux Klan walking through our neighborhood on the holiday of Martin Luther King's birthday and Black History Month. It was a very traumatic experience. They would throw eggs at our house and pig guts on our lawn. Klansmen also walked the streets at night with lit torches.

The first time this happened, my older brothers tried to run them off. But by the time I was thirteen, protecting the home was up to me. Archie and Gregory had already graduated from high school and were on their own.

While my mother worked evenings, I sat in the dining room armed with knives, just in case anyone tried to break into the house and harm my little brother.

It was a very fearful and challenging time for me, but with my father away from home, I knew I had to do everything to protect my family.

Although I was bullied at school, my father demanded that I defend myself.

"Fight back, or you will have to fight me," he said.

Sometimes I would fight back and then run for my life.

Both of my parents taught me to rise above racism and to know that I was not inferior to anyone because of the color of my skin.

My mother taught me the golden rule—to love others despite their bad behavior.

I believe that I was my mother's favorite. She pampered me and was always there with an encouraging word. Later when I was in high school and began running track, my mother would show up to all of my races. For some reason, she didn't want me to play other sports as my older brothers did; she only wanted me to run track. So that's what I did.

God was with me even then, and I didn't know it. I never set my heart on the bitterness of racism. As a matter of fact, many of my friends were white. At times, there was a question in the back of my mind: "Who were those people behind the white mask? Were they the parents of those that I called friends?"

As the years passed, other black families moved into the neighborhood, and we were more readily accepted. By the time I reached junior high school, the classroom was a melting pot.

I always looked up to my older brothers. Gregory was an All American athlete in several sports, and Archie was an All American in track and field, particularly the 400 meter hurdle. By the time I reached my freshmen year at East Jefferson High School, I was ready to follow in their footsteps. I wanted to excel in sports also.

I can remember my first indoor track meet for the 800-meter run. I had trained hard. But as I made my way around the track for the home stretch, I ran out of gas and came in last. I was completely defeated. I can't describe the pain and disappointment I felt to have failed. I spent time alone after the race to lick my wounds.

My father was there, and he was not impressed.

"Junior, it's not in you," he said. "The athletic genes skipped over you. Maybe you should try something else."

I thought, *Man, that's pretty deflating*.

But my coach, Al Nastaci, overheard my father's remarks. He called me into his office the following week.

"I see potential in you. Don't give up," Nastaci told me. "I know what your Dad told you, but the way you worked and trained, if you don't give up, I believe that you will go far."

He said he saw a superstar in me going forward. I was encouraged by his kind words, and I continued to train in track and maintained a 3.0 average.

In my junior year, I moved to Pensacola, Florida, to live with Archie, who was in the air force. He was, and still is, my role model. I attended and ran track at Choctawhatchee High School at Fort Walton Beach, Florida.

I qualified for the state meet in the triple jump, 300-meter hurdle and 400-meter relay. At the state meet I placed fourth in the triple jump, 300-meter hurdles and the 400-meter relay.

My senior year, I returned to East Jefferson High School in Metairie, Louisiana, determined to succeed and earn a track and field scholarship to Louisiana State University.

"This is your year," Nastaci said. "You're going to be the captain of the team, and I want you to take us all the way."

I accepted the challenge. I trained like never before — in the morning before class, after school, and on the weekends.

At the Indoor State Championship, I won first place in the 800-meter and 4x800-meter relay. We came in first place overall and became the 1990 Indoor State Champions, and I received the MVP of the championship. In June of 1990, four members of our team qualified for the Outdoor State Championship (Red O'Laughlin, Robert Thomas, Gerald Bunch, and myself.)

"If you score high enough, we can win the overall state championship," Nastaci said.

No pressure on me, right?

During the race, I paced myself. But as I ran around the last two laps of the track, I threw everything on the line.

I won — we won.

The odds were against us in doing a repeat of the Indoor Championship, but we were able to pull it off and win the Outdoor State Championship as well. No other team from my high school has won the title since then.

Although I considered going to LSU, my heart was to join the air force, like my brother.

But a childhood injury to my eye—a hole in my retina from a stick-ball game—disqualified me. I was disheartened and felt like my world had ended.

One day, when I arrived home from school, I met a Marine Corps recruiter who was standing in my living room.

"So, I hear you want to be a marine?" he said.

"What are you talking about?" I replied. "I did not sign up."

My mother stepped forward.

"Roddy (my nickname), I signed the enlistment card for you," she said.

By this time, my parents had separated. My mother had plans to move to England to live with my older sister, Tonya.

"I want you to be well taken care of," my mother said.

She told me that she was confident that the military could provide a good life for me. I couldn't say no. I admit that I'm a momma's boy.

My mother's love for me has always sustained me. She would often tell me to ignore what others said about me and to follow my heart.

"If it's on the inside of you to do it, pursue it to the best of your ability," she said.

"Yes, Ma'am," I said to her advice.

I signed up for the marines on July 25, 1990.

My coach was disappointed. Together, we had hopes that I might someday compete in the Olympics. He saw that potential in me. But my mother trumps the Olympics!

When I told my father I had joined the marines, he was not pleased.

"Junior, why are you going into the marines? Why aren't you pursuing college?" he asked.

When I told him I was following mom's advice, he took my hand and felt it.

"Junior, you've never done a hard day's work in your life," he said. "There's no way you will make it in the Marine Corps."

I was not discouraged.

"Dad, I'm going. I have to at least try," I told him.

He was deeply disappointed.

But I moved forward. My career with the US military began when I arrived at the Marine Corps Recruit Detachment in San Diego, California, for basic training.

When I started basic training, I was determined to become the best marine I could be. I viewed basic training as a challenge that I could meet and overcome.

I was placed in charge of a squad, and one day we had to go through an obstacle course.

I was elated. I felt happy and go-lucky—it was all in my demeanor. But the drill instructors didn't like it.

"We're going to tear that smile off your face," one drill instructor said to me.

As we made our way through the obstacle course, I climbed a wall and inadvertently placed my hand on a trip wire at the top of the wall.

Suddenly, simulated bombs went off.

"You just got us killed!" the drill instructor yelled at me. "There's no way you're going to make it in the marines. We're going to kick you out. We're going to discharge you."

I was stunned and defeated. I thought, *What a stupid mistake.*

I went back to my barracks after the exercise.

I can't go back home, I thought. *I can't give my father the satisfaction.*

The next morning, the squad stood in formation. The drill instructor was ready for us.

"Some of you are not going to make it," he said. "You might as well pack your bags now. You are a disgrace to the US Marine Corps, so if you know who you are, step forward, pack your bags, and we'll escort you out of here."

I stood tall and firm.

"Recruit Forbes, what are you still doing here?" he asked.

"Drill instructor, I'm going to make a true marine," I said.

"No, you're not."

"Yes, I am, drill instructor."

To reply, the drill instructor smoked the living daylights out of me with intense physical exercise, but I made it. They were creating a lean, mean, fighting machine. I was all in.

While I was in basic training, however, my world turned upside down.

My mother was diagnosed with a malignant brain tumor.

One day, while she was coming home from work, she passed out at the bus stop. I received a Red Cross message about her status. When I requested leave, my platoon leaders were not sympathetic.

"If you leave, you're going to have to re-class and not graduate with your platoon," he said.

"Gunnery sergeant, I have to go. They have only given my mother a few months to live," I replied.

When I got back home, my mother insisted that I return to my platoon.

"Roddy, I'm going to fight this," she said. "You go back and finish strong. I'll be here for you when you graduate."

I gave my mother all the love I had and returned to basic training.

I fought my way back to my platoon and graduated in November 1990 as the most physically fit marine in my class of 371 service members.

My mother was at my graduation, along with my father, who didn't say a word. The gunnery sergeant who said I wouldn't make it was also there. He said he was happy I hadn't quit.

As I look back on those years, I realize he really wanted to see what I was made of. He stayed on me, and by the way, he was from Louisiana.

I was very proud that day.

In November of 1990, I arrived in Cherry Point, North Carolina, at the 2nd Marine Air Wing as a new marine. My job was a 0431, embarkation logistics specialist.

I was on top of the world.

But things soon became chaotic when my mother died on December 9, 1992. It was the lowest point of my life, and I didn't know how to recover from it.

Before she died, I was doing dynamic things for the marines. I was on the all-marine track team, competing against other military services and colleges. But athletics and life didn't matter anymore. I started drinking heavily to get away from the pain and sorrow.

Cpl. Tommy Oatis saw my decline and encouraged me to get my life together.

"I need you to pull out of this," he said to me sternly but with care. "Do you think your mother would want to see you in this manner? I need you to come back. I need you in this fight."

I couldn't continue in this downward spiral. I had to get back in the fight—and I did. I restarted training for track and performing well in my job.

At the end of my marine enlistment in 1994, I was offered a track scholarship from UCLA in the 800-meter.

I decided I wanted to go to college, so I didn't re-enlist. I moved back home to Louisiana to meet my sister, Tonya. We were going to share an apartment in California so I could go to school and my sister could work.

But it didn't happen.

It was close to the start of the school semester, and I had forgone dormitory housing because I planned to live off campus in an apartment. I couldn't afford to live on my own, and without state residency, I could not accept the scholarship.

It was too late in the season for the university to consider my circumstances. So, here I was in Louisiana—no scholarship and no Marine Corps.

What am I going to do? I thought.

I went to the local unemployment office to see if I could get a job with the police force. The human resource specialist asked about my skills. I told her I was a marine and I could maybe be a police officer.

She said that wouldn't work because the police force was crooked, and I seemed like an honest person. It wouldn't work. So, law enforcement was out of the question—or so it seemed.

Gratefully, my cousin Michael Jackson told me about a job as a security guard at the Flamingo Casino. It was the only choice I had, so I took it.

The staff and the regulars at the Casino called me "Robocop." I was no-nonsense and bounced anyone who made trouble. But the environment and the people it drew were not for me.

One day, an army recruiter came to the casino and spotted me right away.

"What are you doing here?" he asked.

I told him how I arrived at the casino and that I had failed my mission.

"Have you ever considered joining the army?" he asked.

He gave me his card, and I later went to his office.

Soon after, I took the US military entrance exam and did well. My new military occupation specialty was in communications.

I signed up for the army in June 1995, and because I was only out of the marines a year, I didn't have to complete basic training.

I went to advanced individual training at Fort Gordon, Augusta, Georgia. By September, I was a newly assigned signal support systems specialist (31U).

My first assignment was with the 2-1 Aviation Battalion in Ansbach, Germany. One day, I was standing in formation, when the first sergeant noticed me.

"Where did you come from, soldier? You stick out like a sore thumb," he said.

I told him that I was once a marine, but I wanted to be the best soldier ever.

He wasn't the only one who noticed me. A short time later, during field training, I caught the eye of Staff Sgt. Patricia Free.

Little did I know that, later, she would become my wife.

It was all the work of the Holy Spirit, and through Patricia, I became a Christian.

My life has been the Lord's ever since.

Chapter Two

THE HOLY SPIRIT SPEAKS

HI, MY NAME IS PATRICIA FORBES. MY HUSBAND IS Command Sgt. Maj. Rodwell Forbes Jr. I thought I would introduce myself because, by God's grace, I have played a very important role in my husband's life.

It was through our relationship that Rodwell gave his life to Christ, and we have been walking together in a Christian life for over twenty years.

Let me tell you a little bit about myself. I was born in Madison, Florida, a small town in the northern region of the state. My parents met in Madison and had an off-and-on marriage. My parents met when my mother was in tenth grade and my father was on furlough from the army. They fell in love the first time they laid eyes on each other.

They wanted to get married, but because my mother was so young, my grandfather said no, naturally. They eloped, and my brother William was born the first year of their marriage. Within another year, I was born.

My father left the army and eventually became a truck driver. After a few years, my parents started having problems, and my father left Florida to work in Philadelphia.

My mother took my brother and me, and we went to live with my aunt in Madison. My grandfather was a Baptist minister and worked at two local churches, one in Madison and the other in Quincy. We lived there for several years, and then my parents reconciled. We moved to Philadelphia to join my father.

During that time, my parents separated frequently. One day, my mother, who was then a housekeeper at a Marriot Hotel, decided to take us children and return to Florida. So, we boarded a Greyhound bus and went back down South. We arrived back in Madison and were met by my aunt.

My father's favorite pastime was going to baseball games, and he took me and my siblings to the Sunday game.

As the years passed and I was in Taylor County High School, my parents could not reconcile their differences, and they finally divorced. But my father attended my high school graduation.

While I was in high school, I was hired as a file clerk at a nearby hospital. I continued to work there after graduation until I enrolled at Tallahassee Community College.

My friend Melody and I started school together, and we began looking for an apartment to share. We found a two-bedroom apartment, and I invited my friend, Brenda, to join us. My mother and my aunt were committed to paying for my rent and food expenses while I studied.

Later on, we met another friend of Brenda's who was serving in the army at Fort Rucker, Alabama. We were all impressed. She had her own apartment and car and lived independent of her parents. I wanted to do the same. I didn't want my mother and aunt to provide for me because I knew it was a burden. But because they loved me, they made the sacrifice.

I asked my mother if I could follow my father's footsteps and enlist in the army. She said to ask him.

"If that's what you want to do, go for it," he said.

So, Brenda, Melanie, and I went to visit an army recruiter in downtown Tallahassee and took the Armed Services Vocational Aptitude Battery (ASVAB). I passed with flying colors and was assigned a job in the clerical field.

We entered into the army through the delayed entry program and did our basic training at Fort Jackson, South Carolina. By August 1979, we were on active-duty. I went to the 71st Lima School for advanced individual training. However, just as we were starting our careers, Melanie left the army to get married.

Soon after, Brenda and I got orders to go to Germany. I didn't want to go. I was a mama's girl, and I didn't want to go anywhere where the people didn't speak English.

We had to take a test before we got our next assignment, and I didn't pass on purpose so I wouldn't have to go to Germany. Instead, I was assigned to Fort Bliss in El Paso, Texas. I got another job assignment 16D HAWK Missile Crewman, and I served there for three years.

Over the next few years, I would serve in Germany with an air defense unit, and then return to Texas. I then went to Germany again and served at Fort Lewis, Washington, for six years. By September 1995, I was a staff sergeant with the 2-1 Aviation Battalion in Ansbach, Germany.

I had also been praying by faith for a husband.

Little did I know that on a training day for soldiers, I would meet him amongst the troops—thanks to the guidance of the Holy Spirit.

I met Specialist Rodwell Forbes Jr. when he walked into the Personnel Administration Center to get his meal card. He was in-processing, and I was working in human resources. He needed a meal card to start his service, but I gave him a hard time because it was after duty hours.

I said, "He can eat off his orders."

Rodwell just stood there looking at me. He didn't say a word. I instructed a soldier to give him his meal card, and we parted ways.

I didn't think about him—no big deal; I was focused on my work. But Rodwell and I were assigned to the same unit, and we both lived on post. I lived in post housing, and he lived in the barracks.

The next time I saw Rodwell, he was standing at attention in formation during a training exercise. I was standing by with a friend, another female soldier.

I happened to glance in Rodwell's direction, and I heard the Holy Spirit say, "That's your husband."

I was surprised and thought, *What? Who?*

I immediately thought nothing of it, but the Holy Spirit spoke again.

"Look over there. That's your husband."

Once again, I glanced over again at Rodwell standing at attention and I thought, *Who, him?*

I couldn't believe it. I knew it was the Holy Spirit, but it didn't make sense.

My husband? I thought to myself. "Who? Him?" I asked.

"Yes, him. That's your husband," the Holy Spirit said.

Well, I didn't know what to think. I wasn't paying Rodwell any mind. I was thinking of my work and raising my two daughters, La'Tisha and La'Shauna.

But the day after the training, the Holy Spirit directed me to invite Rodwell to my church's anniversary celebration. I thought, *How could this happen?*

I had been married before and was raising two children on my own. I was a higher rank than Rodwell and was considered a supervisor. I also later learned that I was twelve years older than him.

But I followed the Holy Spirit's instructions.

I later went to the arms room to clean my weapon and was going downstairs to the basement. Rodwell was walking up the stairs. We were the only people on the stairwell. He had a big smile on his face as usual; how strange I thought that was.

I didn't know if he would say yes, or if he even attended church, but I stopped and asked him. He immediately said yes, and his response caught me off guard.

That was too easy, I thought.

"I don't have a car," he said.

I did. I told him that I would pick him up on Saturday.

When I arrived, Rodwell was wearing the only suit he owned. At church, Rodwell thought he could sit next to me, but I was a leader at my church and that was not allowed.

Rodwell was not a saved Christian, and he didn't know what it meant to be one. Eventually, I learned that he was living a party life. When Rodwell recalls this time in his life, he said this was the way he grew up.

I saw the evidence of his lifestyle when I picked him up for church on Sunday. He was not presentable. He had partied hard the night before.

I thought, *This is a different person.* But the Holy Spirit kept speaking to me in my prayer time.

"You're doing the right thing. He needs to hear My Word," the Holy Spirit said.

A few weeks later, Rodwell told me that he was volunteering to deploy to Bosnia. He told me that when he arrived there, he would call and write to me.

I thought, *Yeah, right. We don't really know each other.*

But true to his word, I received a phone call and a letter.

The Holy Spirit told me that our relationship would blossom by faith. We kept communicating by phone and letter. Sometimes it was

17

good, sometimes not. But by October 1996, I learned that I had to deploy to Bosnia on a special assignment to be a supervisor at the brigade level.

I was mad and hurt. I didn't want to leave my girls, but I had to go. Some women and friends from my church helped me pack up my house, and I decided to send my daughters to Florida to live with my family.

I arrived in Bosnia and ironically saw Rodwell on Thanksgiving Day for about thirty minutes, and then he was gone. By December, Rodwell was back in Germany to attend a leadership school. While he was there, he kept writing and calling.

But Rodwell had a girlfriend on the side. Soldiers in Germany who were my friends would contact me and tell me how they saw him with the woman—sometimes holding hands.

I wasn't happy. I thought he was talking out of two sides of his mouth, and I didn't like what he was saying. By April 1997, I decided it was over for me.

He arrived back in Bosnia, and when he saw me, he said, "You can at least give me a hug."

I was furious.

"No, you're nasty," I told him. "In the mud with all these girls."

"What do you mean?" he said.

I couldn't believe it. He couldn't man up and tell me truth.

Later on, for some reason, he gave me his black pouch for me to hold. He carried it everywhere.

I thought, *There's something in this pouch that I need to know about.*

I decided to take a look inside the black pouch. I found train tickets that Rodwell had purchased to visit the girl in Germany.

I guess it's true, I thought to myself.

All of my military friends were warning me about Rodwell in letters from Bosnia and Germany. They thought I was golden and felt they could choose someone for me.

The Holy Spirit continued to speak to me. When Rodwell first deployed, I was instructed to send him care packages, which I did. I thought Rodwell was a person who needed to know the Lord.

I prayed to the Lord to release me from Rodwell.

"Let him go," I heard the Holy Spirit say.

It felt like a ton of bricks were lifted off my shoulders.

"Here's your pouch," I told Rodwell. "I'm done with you. You embarrass me in the Lord's name."

He was shocked. He didn't believe me.

I went back to work, only to see him in my office later that day. He was looking pitiful, and he asked if we could talk.

"I'm going nowhere with you," I said.

He just stood there looking stunned and hurt. I told him I would only speak to him inside the post chapel.

I thought, *He's not brave enough to lie to me in God's house.*

So we met at the post chapel and talked. I asked him if he was a saved Christian.

"Sure, I'm saved," he said.

He told me that he read a chapter of the Bible every day, that he was nice to people, and that he tried to do a good deed every day.

"Have you accepted Jesus Christ as your Lord and Savior?"

He said no.

"Then that makes you a good sinner who would blast hell wide open," I said.

The chapel's minister came to pray with us, and I asked Rodwell if he wanted to accept Jesus as his Savior. He said yes.

I read Romans 10:8-11, and Rodwell made his confession. He accepted Jesus right then and there.

It was midnight—the eve of Easter morning in 1997. We attended the sunrise Easter service together and took Holy Communion. The chaplain guided us together in the faith as we later attended church and Bible study. He was a man who loved the Lord and was there for us.

Since we were both saved in Christ, the idea of marriage seemed possible. But ironically, while we were in Germany, Rodwell asked me to marry him twice—over the phone. I said no both times.

But in May 1997, he formally proposed on bended knee. I accepted after being treated to dinner and receiving a gift of Oscar de la Renta perfume. I wanted to say yes to him in person—eye to eye.

Soon after our engagement, we both applied for leave so we could get married in Florida. We decided to go to Florida since my girls were there and Rodwell's brother Archie lived there. Our plan was to get married by the justice of the peace.

When we arrived in Florida, I went to my Aunt Ann's house, and Rodwell went to Archie's.

Two days later, Rodwell called and told me he was going to pick me and the girls up so I could get a wedding dress. I was surprised. He also said we would be married in Archie's church. I had prayed that if I ever did remarry, I wanted to have a church wedding. But Rodwell knew nothing of my heart's desire.

Well, the next day, Rodwell and I signed the paperwork for our marriage license.

On July 26, 1997, we were married, and Rodwell's father gave me away. His sister-in-law was my maid of honor, and my daughters were my flower girls. We had our reception at Fort Walton Beach.

When we returned to Germany, we had another reception at my church.

I was so happy. I thought, *God, you're showing out.*

I had no idea that two years before, when the Holy Spirit said "That's your husband," I would be so blessed.

Chapter Three

THE ARMY LIFE – PART ONE

AFTER THE WEDDING, MY NEW WIFE, FAMILY, AND I returned to Ansbach, Germany. We returned to the 2-1 Aviation Battalion, and I pressed forward in my life as a new Christian.

I was enthusiastic in my new faith, and I took it seriously. I left my old life behind. In earlier conversations, I told Patricia about all my bad choices. I held no secrets from her, for I was committed to a life in Jesus Christ.

But not everyone believed in my conversion. Ministers in our church, the Church of God in Christ, which was located off the installation, were skeptical of me.

My old running buddies laughed when I no longer participated in negative behaviors. They thought it was a phase that I was going through. But they were wrong.

I was a Bible-thumping, God-fearing, evangelizing Christian. I would walk up to anyone—even a complete stranger—and ask them if they knew the Good News of the gospel of Jesus Christ and tried my best to bring as many to Christ as possible.

It was a time of acceptance and rejection for me.

While people were critical of me, I was critical of leaders in the church who I thought were not living their lives according to the teachings of Jesus Christ.

But God laid His word on my heart and asked me, "What manner of man are you?"

I answered God by promising I would strive to be faithful and obedient in my walk with Christ—a vow I continue to live by today.

I was encouraged, and my wife and I worked together to help build a new church—Living Water Ministries Church in Ansbach.

During the next four years of my army career, I would be deployed to Sarajevo, Tuzla, and Katterbach, Germany, where I served with the 7-1 Aviation Battalion and 2-1 Aviation Battalion.

As the year 2002 approached, the decade mark of my career, I was considering whether to separate from the army and devote my life to the ministry. But as I struggled with my decision, I learned that I was on the list to be promoted to sergeant first class.

One day, when Patricia and I were returning home from Bible study and had stopped by McDonald's for an ice cream sundae, I asked her what she thought about my decision to get out of the military.

She said, "God showed me that you will be a command sergeant major, and sergeant major of the army is yours if you want it."

The sergeant major of the army is the highest ranking enlisted non-commissioned officer in the service branch.

The decision was made. I would stay in the army.

The associates at our new church were disappointed, but this was what I was called to do. But before moving forward, I was ordained as a minister.

By fate, the day I re-enlisted was the worst day in our country's history—September 11, 2001. Immediately, as the World Trade Center in New York was attacked, our unit went on shut down. We knew we would go to war.

I was a platoon sergeant at the time. I was shocked to learn that the unit's first sergeant did not want to deploy. As a matter of fact, he cried when he learned that we would do so.

His cowardice shocked and insulted me. I lost all respect for him. I told the unit commander that I would not support him.

"We need another first sergeant," I suggested.

"We don't have another first sergeant," the commander said.

"Then I'll be the first sergeant," I said.

That was not going to happen, because we already had a first sergeant in position. So, being a soldier, I followed orders and got on board.

Patricia retired from the army as a sergeant first class in 2002, and soon after, I got orders to 2/502nd, an infantry battalion, 101st Airborne Division at Fort Campbell, Kentucky.

I was a sergeant first class and was assigned as the commo chief to help with training as the unit prepared to deploy. We eventually deployed as part of Operation Iraqi Freedom and served for twelve months.

We were charged with establishing the lines of communication for army camps in the field. As a commo platoon, we went above and beyond the call of duty and did a phenomenal job.

When we returned to the states, our platoon was acknowledged as the best in the battalion by the command sergeant major (CSM).

It was very difficult for a non-infantry soldier to receive a Bronze Star Medal because you had to go above and beyond the call of duty, and we did just that. We took over the combat logistics patrol, which escorted food trucks to different forward operating bases for life line support. This task was normally supported by the infantry, but the commo platoon was up for the task. We did an exceptional job, resulting in the infantry units being freed up to fight the enemy's tactics.

The Bronze Star Medal is given to United States Armed Forces personnel for bravery, acts of merit, or meritorious service, according to the Bronze Star Medal website.

The sergeant major later asked me to serve with the 4th Brigade Combat Team at Fort Campbell to help build it up for another deployment to Iraq.

I said yes.

I was not only a disciple for Christ, but I was also a disciple of physical fitness. My years as an athlete in high school established a habit and foundation of consistent exercise, which remains a part of my life.

The sergeant major, who was later on the list for brigade CSM, asked me to screen the soldiers for physical fitness. I did, and I worked to whip our soldiers in shape for the mission ahead.

In time, I learned that there was a first sergeant position open. There were several master sergeants who were eligible, but they were not hungry for the position. I was.

I went to the sergeant major and asked if I could fill the position.

"Yes, you can," he said. "But I still need you to be the commo chief."

I said, "Yes, sir, I will."

I was pumped up!

The next morning, when I went out to the formation of my soldiers, I proudly told them to come to attention.

Everyone did as expected, except some of the master sergeants. One of the master sergeants dared to walk away from the formation. I called him out and told him I was the new first sergeant and no one walks away from the formation.

He kept on walking.

I went to the see the Sergeant Major.

"There's a mutiny in the ranks, and I need to know that you have my back because some of these senior NCOs do not want to come on board," I told him.

The next day, he went out to the formation and told them that I was the first sergeant and if anyone had problem with me, they would have a problem with him.

"First sergeant, take care of your formation," he said.

After a year of training, we got our orders to deploy to Iraq. I was honored and excited.

I was the Headquarters and Headquarters Company first sergeant a infantry combat brigade—how often does that happen?

However, before we left for Iraq, I walked into my office one day and saw another first sergeant standing there.

"What are you doing in my office?" I asked.

"I'm the new first sergeant," he said.

"The new first sergeant where?"

"I'm the new first sergeant here," he replied.

"And who approved that?" I asked.

"The sergeant major."

I went to see the sergeant major.

"Say it isn't so. There's a first sergeant in my office," I said.

"Yes," he said. "Human Resources Command sent him in, and I have to take him because you're not promotable."

I was not considered promotable because I had not served the required amount of time as a sergeant first class in order to be promoted.

"I understand that. But the thing that bothers me is that you didn't tell me, and that is like you slapped me in the face," I said respectfully.

"But you're still in a master sergeant position as the commo chief of the brigade," he said.

"Yes," I said. I was badly hurt, but I soldiered on.

We deployed to Iraq. This was my second deployment in support of Operation Iraqi Freedom. While we were there, the first sergeant was relieved of his position and replaced by someone else.

Soon after, I became promotable, and when the replacement was relieved of his position, I became the first sergeant.

But before coming back to the states, I learned that I would have to give up my first sergeant position because it was only a twelve-month assignment.

I told the Human Resources Command that I was not giving up my diamond rank and that I would seek out a viable first sergeant position on my own. I reached out to the G1 at Fort Bragg, and by divine appointment, I was able to get in contact with a very close friend of ours who worked there, Katrina Elbert. She told me about a 1SG position that was open and gave me the information to reach out to them.

I found out that the 586th Signal Company at Fort Bragg, North Carolina, needed a first sergeant to build up the unit as I had done at Fort Campbell and that they were going to deploy to Iraq.

I spoke to the brigade command sergeant major. He told me to send my paperwork, but he would not take me unless I spoke to my wife and family because I was already deployed and should take time to decompress and spend quality time with them.

"Your wife must agree with it," he told me.

Patricia, who was living in North Carolina, gave me her blessing.

"If that's what you want to do, do it," she said.

So, I came back to the states and headed to Fort Bragg and briefly trained the company before we were deployed out to Iraq.

We did what we needed to do for the mission and brought everyone back safely.

I'm proud to say that during my three deployments to Iraq, I not only served as a soldier, but I also remained sensitive to the guidance of the Holy Spirit and established three churches in Iraq. Many soldiers and Iraqi nationals gave their lives to Christ as a result.

While I was in Iraq, I promised Patricia that I would take an assignment stateside in order to be there for her and the family.

I called the Human Resources Command while I was still deployed and told them that I wanted to be a senior military science instructor for the Army Reserve Officers' Training Corps (ROTC).

I wanted to be an ROTC instructor because during my time as a platoon sergeant and first sergeant, I wondered why the second lieutenants who graduated from ROTC were not properly prepared for duty.

The Human Resources Command said that I was not qualified for the position because my military occupation specialty was not combat arms.

There was an ROTC position available at Hampton University in Virginia, and I wanted it. I spoke to the command sergeant major of the ROTC program. He said I had the position, but I couldn't fail.

"I'm putting my reputation on the line for you," he said.

So, when I returned to the states in 2008, I headed to Hampton University. When I arrived, I discovered that the morale and mentality of the ROTC cadets were substandard.

There was a competition called the Ranger Challenge, which was described as the "varsity sport" of ROTC. The battalion's top cadets competed against teams from other colleges and universities. Events included patrolling, marksmanship, weapons assembly, a one-rope bridge, a grenade assault course, an army physical fitness test, land navigation, and a ten-kilometer road march. The event was held at Fort Bragg, North Carolina.

The ROTC cadets under my charge did not feel they could win because they were African Americans and couldn't stand up to the other college students.

I told the ROTC lieutenant colonel I could turn that around if he supported me. He said he would, and I went to work right away—starting with the cadre of ROTC instructors to change the culture and the mindset of the leaders in the ROTC program.

Within a year, the cadets were holding their heads up high and were proud to be cadets of the "Pirate Battalion."

Even though they didn't win the overall competition, they scored the highest in the school's history, and they continue to climb the ladder.

Although the assignment at Hampton University was for three years, I was only there a year because I learned that I was on the promotion list for sergeant major.

I attended the sergeant major academy in El Paso, Texas, for a year. By 2010, I was the command sergeant major of AFSouth in Naples, Italy. Unfortunately, in this position, I was often away on training and left Patricia at home alone.

While we were in Italy, a curious thing happened. When we looked out our window or ventured outside our home, men in cars would drive by honking their horns.

We thought they were being friendly.

But our neighbors soon told us that African women in Naples were often approached to be hired as prostitutes. The drivers were not being neighborly. They thought they could hire Patricia as an escort!

For a year, Patricia diligently prayed to get us out of Naples. There was no way I could go away on trainings and leave her in such a vulnerable position.

As God would have it, we left Italy in one year instead of the three-year assignment. We headed to Germany and left the dangers of Italy behind us.

Chapter Three

THE ARMY LIFE- PART TWO

MY NEXT ASSIGNMENT WAS AS THE COMMAND SER-geant major for the 72nd Expeditionary Signal Battalion in Schweinfurt, Germany in 2012.

When I arrived for duty, I learned that the battalion was in disarray and the soldiers were out of control. It was considered the most ill-disciplined battalion in the 5th Signal Command.

My predecessor told me, "Forbes, you were put into this position for a reason. Now it's yours, and you have to fix it."

I had a job on my hands. I soon found out that some of the battalion's soldiers were gang members, drug dealers, and pimps who ran a prostitution ring. And believe it or not, rapes were being committed in the barracks.

I was shocked. How could this criminal activity be going on inside an army unit? We had to change the entire atmosphere.

That is when I developed my philosophy of Dignity, Integrity, Motivation, and Empowerment (DIME).

I told the commander that I needed his support to weed out the bad elements and have them disciplined immediately. So, with his support,

I started nighttime surveillance operations along with the S-3 sergeant major to catch the criminals at their game.

During formation, I told the soldiers that we were going after the criminals in the battalion and their associates. As soon as our efforts began, my phone began to ring throughout the night with news about the progress of the operations.

It took two years, but eventually the criminals were weeded out and received the appropriate punishments. Some were stripped of their rank and pay, and some were discharged.

We also worked to heighten the morale and motivation of the soldiers in the organization. We spent some quality time sprucing up the unit by beautifying the grounds, and what had looked like a jungle soon became as pristine as a golf course.

In time, the battalion became one of the most sought-after battalion in the Command. With God's help, we were able to turn things around and improve the battalion's reputation.

Eventually, however, the unit was deactivated in 2014. My last assignment was as the command sergeant major at Fort Meade in Maryland.

I went from being responsible for about 800 soldiers in the battalion to having to help oversee what is now the second largest army installation by population with a workforce of 56,000 active-duty service members, Department of Defense civilians, and contractors.

It was mind blowing. But God told me, "If you continue to have a humble spirit before me and the people you are serving, I will give you a larger platform."

It was great teaming up with the garrison commander, who was the face and voice of the installation; I was the eyes and ears.

I called him "The Professor" because of his ability to articulate Fort Meade's mission as the nation's pre-eminent intelligence center and meticulously advocate for resources with the installation's growth.

Fort Meade is the home of the National Security Agency, the Defense Information Systems Agency, and Cyber and Military Intelligence Commands.

I was "The Closer." I brought the commander's message home to the garrison's leaders and employees. I was also the colonel's eyes and ears. I established relationships within the Fort Meade community to have an idea of the pulse of the people we served, those we worked with, and those that lived on post.

When the former garrison commander ended his tenure in 2016, I then worked with the new garrison commander.

In *Soundoff*, the installation's weekly army newspaper, an article was published for my retirement in 2017, in which the former garrison commander called me "one of the best noncommissioned officers" he had worked with during his army career.

His successor said he was "proud to have worked with one of the army's absolute best senior leaders."

I was grateful for their kind words. It touched my heart that two of my battle buddies would honor me with such compliments.

One of the highlights of my time at Fort Meade was the installation's partnership with Hospice of the Chesapeake, a nonprofit organization based in Pasadena, Maryland, that provides palliative and hospice care.

Shortly after I arrived at Fort Meade, Diane Sancillo, the director of Volunteer Services at the organization, contacted me to ask if the installation could provide service members to participate in its Honor Salute Program. The program honors military veterans who are hospice patients.

I was more than happy to help. Once the details were cleared by our Office of the Staff Judge Advocate, Fort Meade's service members began to participate through the army's Volunteer Corps Program.

An Honor Salute happens when a group of service men and women literally give a group of veterans a salute of honor. On March 30, 2015, I was asked to lead the Honor Salute for the organization's first annual Welcome Home Vietnam Veterans Day observance. On that day, Maryland Governor Lawrence Hogan signed legislation establishing it as Welcome Home Vietnam Veterans Day. The law acknowledges the service and sacrifice of service members who fought in the Vietnam War during the 1960s and 1970s.

I was also asked to be the guest speaker at the observance. The entire event sparked something in my heart. Unfortunately, when many service members returned from the Vietnam War, they were not treated with the same respect as veterans from other US conflicts. Historians note that Vietnam veterans were spat upon and called "baby killers" by their own countrymen.

At the event, many Vietnam veterans shared their stories with me, and I was deeply saddened and angry. I decided then that I would do everything I could to advocate for them to receive the recognition and respect they were due and the services and supports that they deserved.

My partnership with Hospice of the Chesapeake continues. In 2017, I was the guest speaker and led the Honor Salute, and I also led last year's Honor Salute.

On June 14, 2017, I had my retirement ceremony for serving twenty-seven years in the army.

The garrison held a retirement ceremony for me at Fort Meade's McGill Training Center. Patricia, my father, my siblings, and my children and grandchildren attended the ceremony, along with several former colleagues and battle buddies.

The ceremony included kind words and well wishes from Maj. Gen. Phillip Churn, currently the assistant to the chairman of the joint chiefs of staff, Reserve Matters; Lt. Col. Darcy Saint-Amant, deputy brigade commander of the 21st Signal Brigade at Fort Detrick; and my brother Archie Aples, Hertford's North Carolina city councilman.

An "Old Glory" ceremony was held, and I was presented an American flag. I also received the Legion of Merit.

To my surprise, Patricia purchased a new truck for me and showed me a picture of the vehicle on her iPad during the ceremony.

What can I say? It was one of the most memorable and emotional days of my life.

After the ceremony, Patricia and I said goodbye to Fort Meade and the army and headed to our new home in Raeford, North Carolina.

How sweet it is!

Chapter Four

A New Calling

During my tenure as the senior enlisted adviser at Fort Meade and my partnership with the Hospice of the Chesapeake, my life was changed once again. I now have a new calling and purpose that, with God's help, I am determined to fulfill.

As I have already mentioned, on March 30, 2015, I led the Honor Salute for the Hospice of the Chesapeake's first annual Welcome Home Vietnam Veterans Day observance. On that day, I met a Vietnam veteran who talked to me about the impact the war had on his life. In our conversation, he told me that I would "be a fool" if I did not take advantage of the services the army provides to soldiers to help them deal with the hardships of combat and deployments. He said that I should do so before I retired.

I was struck by his words; it was like he hit me upside my head with a stack of bricks.

Although I did not fully realize it at the time, I was physically, emotionally, and spiritually suffering from my decade-long experience of back-to-back deployments during my twenty-seven years of service.

From 1996 to 2009, I went on ten deployments and four combat and six peace keeping missions. In 2002, I began three deployments to Iraq during Operation Iraqi Freedom.

My first deployment was for a year. I came home for eight months and was deployed again for fifteen months. Then, I came home again for nine months and was deployed for a year.

As a soldier, I experienced the horrors of war. With my battle buddies, I endured offensive and defensive attacks. We had to be in a high state of readiness all the time—24/7, every day. Although I was never physically wounded, praise God, and remained in prayer for myself and the soldiers under my watch, I did have a soldier critically wounded, and I was almost hit by a sniper's fire and blown up by improvised explosive devices (IED's) numerous times. Thankfully, I can say that I never lost a soldier under my watch in the field. It was only because of God's hedge of protection that this was able to happen.

We heard about post-traumatic stress disorder during our time in Iraq. At that time, the word was that it was similar to the "shell shock" that service members in Vietnam experienced.

Honestly, I didn't put much real estate in it. Every time I returned to the states and went to medical for my re-entry exam, I was asked about my mental state.

"Fine, sir, no problem," was my reply. I wanted to return fit and ready to go back out in the field if need be.

I didn't realize it then, but each time I came back from a deployment, parts of me never returned.

By the time my deployments ended in 2009, I had started to descend down a spiral of addiction and emotional torment that lasted until my diagnosis of chronic post-traumatic stress disorder, traumatic brain injury and borderline bipolar disorder in 2016.

I was living a double life. To the outside world, I was a soldier—fit for duty and able to give and follow commands. But when I returned home to my wife and family, I was a wreck. I lived in isolation and seclusion.

I would come home, bury myself in silence, and drink wine until I blacked out. When I did manage to sleep, it would only be for two to three hours. In the middle of the night, I would wake up in a sweat, frightened by dreams of demons and people trying to ambush me in the field.

Sometimes I would jump out of bed to try to take cover. The slightest noise would remind me of a bomb going off.

In the morning, I would manage to pull myself together, determined to fulfill my duties as a soldier—and I did.

No one knew about my suffering—no one except Patricia. My poor wife witnessed it all. As I climbed the ladder of career success, my wife diligently prayed over and protected me. When I wasn't coherent, she kept people away from our home after duty hours.

And unfortunately, she also suffered in silence. Although I was never violent, Patricia became a prisoner in her own home. Why? She seldom left home to run errands or visit friends because she didn't know what manner of man I would be when she returned.

"You give your all to your job," she told me. "Everyone else is receiving the best of you, but I'm not. The children are not, and the grandchildren are not. You need help."

But I was in denial. I thought as long as I functioned as a soldier, I was fine. I showed no weaknesses, so I had no weaknesses.

My family also suffered because in my silence, I never expressed my true feelings. I told people what I thought they wanted to hear. I was numb to my own emotions. I couldn't connect with the people I loved. I wasn't emotionally or spiritually present to give them the love and support they deserved.

My father and siblings had no idea what was going on under my roof. My brother Archie knew I drank, but he didn't know how much.

I was losing my family.

When I heard the words of that Vietnam veteran, a light bulb went off in my head.

I needed to seek help.

So, I made an appointment with a psychiatrist and psychologist in the behavioral health division at Kimbrough Ambulatory Care Center, the medical facility at Fort Meade.

The counsel I received was not wise counsel. When I told the mental health providers about my experiences and symptoms, I was told that I was having a "midlife crisis."

I was shocked.

"Do you mean to tell me that after everything I've told you, all you can say to me is that I'm having a midlife crisis?" I said with irritation.

"Well, sergeant major. I always see you around the garrison," said the psychiatrist. "You seem fine."

I was also discouraged because over time, the psychologist began to seek my counsel!

"Well, there's no need for me to talk to you," I said.

I asked for a referral to professionals off the installation. I eventually met with a psychiatrist and psychologist once every two weeks.

At first, the psychologist told me that she was skeptical as to whether I had a mental health issue. But as she pulled back the layers of my life, from childhood forward, my issues surfaced.

I underwent an intensive eight-phase study that examined me medically, psychologically, and emotionally. The result was my diagnosis.

The discovery has given me a new calling.

I am now working to educate service members and veterans about mental health issues and addictions, and I advocate on their behalf to ensure that they receive appropriate treatment and care they so rightfully deserve. I also hope to inspire and empower them to live their lives to the fullest so that they may fulfill God's destiny for them.

I've decided to let my life be an open door—which is why I have written this book. I am striving to be an example to anyone in uniform that they can overcome any obstacle and live a life of purpose and meaning.

I celebrate who I am in Christ, and each day I am victorious!

I was prescribed medication for my mental health issues and to help me sleep, but the medications did not agree with me.

I have sleep apnea and have been using a continuous positive airway device to help with my breathing at night, and now I sleep better and longer.

I am not only getting better physically, but emotionally too.

Patricia and I are on this journey together, and now that I am retired, we are getting to know each other better. I am opening up, expressing my emotions, and Patricia is sharing her love of laughter. My wife is a comedian—and I love it!

Not that I don't struggle some days—because I do. But I don't walk in condemnation. I walk in God's grace.

As a military leader and a Christian, I know that other leaders and people of faith may be reluctant to come forward to get help for a mental health disorder or addiction. I understand. I once thought that and allowed pride and fear to get into the way. I thought I had to have it all together and I just had to do more to become better. I had to be spot on; there was no room for error.

But if I didn't have Christ in my life, I don't know that I would have come forward. I know the Word of God tells us to be honest with Him about what goes on in our hearts. So, we must be honest with ourselves.

And we must know that God has provided a way for us to deal with and overcome our struggles. These are issues that cannot be "prayed" away. I must be willing to put some action behind it.

Jesus is the ultimate healer, but He has given gifts and talents to professionals who can help us to heal with His grace and mercy.

There is help and appropriate care for those who seek help. And if you, like me, feel you're not getting the help you need or deserve, speak up! Stand up for yourself and don't give up until you do!

I am dedicated to doing everything I can to ensure that service members and veterans who have sacrificed their lives for this country are given the very best. They deserve it, "You" deserve it!

To gain the skills to help others in need, I became a motivational speaker and a certified life coach. I decided to become a life coach because over the past twenty-seven years in the military, I've had the privilege to counsel thousands of service members, civilians, and their families. I understand that credentialing means a lot in the civilian sector, which is why I pursued this profession.

As a life coach, I provide a myriad list of services. For example, the acronym "SPYRAL" describes the areas that I specialize in: **S**piritual Renewal, **P**ost Traumatic Stress Disorder, **Y**outh, **R**ediscover Your Destiny, **A**ddictions, and **L**eadership.

I am truly passionate about people becoming everything they were created to be.

The overall goal for my new business is to spread awareness about mental illnesses and encourage others to seek the proper care that is available for them. You no longer have to suffer in silence. Let your voice be heard because you just don't know how it may help someone else.

The message I would like to give to all is that there is no weakness in coming forward with a mental illness. It takes great strength to acknowledge the problem and seek the appropriate help that is readily available. Once again, I've been diagnosed with chronic PTSD, traumatic brain injury (TBI) and borderline bipolar disorder, and I've been seeking professional help and attending therapeutic classes with people who have the same struggles. I've found that the more open I am with talking about mental illness, the more I'm able to deal with it.

There may not be a cure for PTSD as of yet, but the treatments can help us navigate through life's struggles and challenges. Not only do you and I deserve to feel better, but those who are closest to us deserve the same. I've found that the family members of the mentally ill often suffer in silence because they have to cover and shelter their loved ones.

On September 1, 2017, I retired from the United States Army after serving 27 years. I have learned so much about myself—who I truly am and what I'm passionate about doing. For the past twenty-seven years, my life conformed to the ways of the military, and I became everything that they wanted me to be.

I'm not saying that's a bad thing, but somewhere along the line, I put myself to the side and personified the "selfless service" that the military requires of service members.

Now that I'm retired, I've learned to live a balanced life of both "selfless service" and "selfish service." What do I mean by "selfish service?" You have to take time out for yourself because if you don't, you can lose your identity and find yourself just going through the motions.

The army drills into soldiers' minds that we must be selfless in the things that we do, but I do believe that you have to be balanced because when it's all said and done, the military will continue to go on, with or without you. When you leave the military, you're left with yourself trying to integrate into the civilian community.

Once I realized this, doing the things that I truly enjoy has been an awesome experience, and that's been encouraging and inspiring people to become the best that they are destined to be. I wish you the best on this life journey and just know that you can do all things through Christ who strengthens you.

Have a Blessed, Fruitful and Overcoming day on Purpose!!

Resource Guide

This book is only the first step in the journey to your recovery. While I am a life coach, I am not a mental health or addiction professional, and there are national resources available that can help you. Here is a partial listing of resources that may be of assistance to you. Remember, you deserve to be happy and healthy. Let these professionals help you take the first step to a life of purpose and joy.

National Center for Post-Traumatic Stress Disorder – US Department of Veterans Affairs
1-844-698-2311

National Suicide Prevention Lifeline
1-800-273-8255

Suicide Prevention Army G-1 Human Resources
1-800-273-8255
www.armyg1.army.mil

Suicide Prevention US Navy
www.suicide.navy.mil

Suicide Prevention Air Force
703-697-3039
www.af.mil/suicide-prevention

Suicide Prevention Coast Guard
1-855-247-8778
www.dcms.uscg.mil-suicide-prevention-program

Helping Adult Depression
www.treat-major-depression.com

Depression and Bipolar Support Alliance
1-800-826-3822

Schizophrenia-Make the Connection – US Department of
Veterans Affairs
https://maketheconnection.net

National Alliance on Mental Illness
www.nami.org
1-800-950-6264

National Addiction Hotline
1-877-205-6625

CPSIA information can be obtained
at www.ICGtesting.com
Printed in the USA
BVHW040151060319
541892BV00005B/23/P